The Dusk of Exile

Jila Mossaed

The Dusk of Exile

Poems of Longing and Light

Selected & Translated by

Mojdeh Bahar

MAGE PUBLISHERS

Mage Publishers Inc
www.mage.com

Library of Congress Cataloging-in-Publication Data
Available at the Library of Congress

ISBN 978-1-949445-96-1

Email: as@mage.com •
Mage online: www.mage.com

To the memory of Claudette Sartiliot

Contents

Introduction

Jila Mossaed Estakhri (known professionally as Jila Mossaed) is an award-winning Swedish-Iranian poet and writer who was elected to the Swedish Academy in 2018. Born in Tehran in 1948, she pursued her studies in Iran and the United States and remained in Iran until 1985. She wrote her first poems at the age of twelve and published her first poem at the age of seventeen. Her first poetry collection, *Ghazālān-e Chālāk-e Khātereh* (The fast gazelles of memory) was published in Tehran before she emigrated to Sweden. The remaining ten Persian poetry collections have been published in Sweden.

After settling in Sweden she made a decision to write poetry in Swedish as well as her native Persian. Her first poetry collection in Swedish was published in 1997. She has since written nine other poetry collections in Swedish for which she has won numerous awards. Her most recent collection was published earlier this year. In addition to poetry, Mossaed has written three novels, *Panjereh-ee Bāz Ru Beh Khābhā-ye Qadimi* (An open window facing old dreams) *Ishtār*, *Tufān* (Storm); a children's book and over 60 articles.

Mossaed has built a distinguished career writing in both Persian and Swedish. Her poetry and prose have been translated into English, French, Greek, and Dutch, introducing her voice to a global readership.

Spanning five decades, her Persian poetry meditates on themes of life and death, womanhood, love, home, exile, nostalgia, and aging. Her singular voice fuses inner landscapes with the outer world, weaving the natural environment and its elements into the fabric of human experience.

Mossaed's work holds a unique place in literary history: she is not only a vital figure in both Persian and Swedish letters but also the first member of the Swedish Academy born in Iran. This book celebrates her as a poet of exile and belonging, of memory and renewal—an author who bridges cultures and enriches the global literary scene.

Translator's Note

I first learned about Jila Mossaed's poetry leafing through a publication by a local Persian literary magazine. The small volume captured a handful of women poets. I later learned that the poets had gathered in the Washington D.C. area in the 1990s and the magazine had subsequently decided to publish some of their poetry.

Years later, I set out to do an anthology of contemporary Iranian women poets, and went to search for Jila Mossaed. I contacted her and obtained her permission to translate a few of her poems for the anthology, *Song of the Ground Jay*.

We kept in touch, and I asked if I could translate more of her work. Thankfully, she agreed and the current selection captures poems from each of the eleven Persian collections, arranged in reverse chronological order.

From the Collection

To the Face of the Moon

Sweden, 2022

We have misinterpreted the world
since the beginning

The bird has never sung for us
The moon doesn't know that it shines
The flowers are unaware of their own
  colors and scents

Nature is blind to our existence
and doesn't know how, from fear,
deep in the cave
We have created a faceless monster
Who'll never let us go.

Upon day's arrival
My small balcony
sends me a message
to open the door

The faded sunlight of exile
doesn't let me remember that
the shadow of a cloud
Is always waiting in a corner
to rain on
precious moments of recollection.

No covering has kept me warm
All these years
I've gone naked

Yellow sunlight
Radiant green earth
Short summer days
Did not help
It was as if no piece of clothing
fit me

I wrapped
The sky
The woods
The mountains
Around me
Yet, I did not feel warm

Except the moments
when the warm breeze
would
touch my face
and the scent of the past would permeate the room
Otherwise
In the frost of loneliness
I would've turned into an icicle
in the cave of years long past.

Her parti-colored skirt
shrouded my morning slumber
A mother who was not happy
A woman who thought of giving birth
as duty
died hoping for love

O vast multitude of waiting mothers
Come out of
that small dark room
Make a knot in time
Return to your youth
And experience
Love

I wish they'd draw lanes
for finding the path to love
And place signs on the road of feelings
So no lovers
would lose their way.

If time had a ceiling
If the walls crumbled
If love arrived unmasked
I'd throw away this old dress

Poetry is my wine
Poetry's been my wine
throughout my life

Calming
Amnesia-inducing
Chasing away the blues

If poetry didn't exist
Wine
would keep me in its heaven

Between two tall walls
Two narrow corridors
I stand

A wall of words
A wall of time
A wall of madness
A wall of pain
Two runaway trains
Thunder above my head
I scream
No one hears me

Maybe
This is
the eternal place

This soil
is polluted
This earth
is rotten
Water's drowned in water
The seas have collapsed into themselves

The earth's intelligence has diminished
Where will you plant the bombs?
Where will they thrive?
The earth is angry
It no longer trusts us
The doors of secrets were shut in our face,
yet we had wrested a promise from Time.
Suspended
In mid air
to destroy what we have built
we must search for its cause.

Before I could recognize letters
Before words took shape in my throat
My language was that of a tree

My mother's language
was the limpid language of milk
flowing through veins

The mother tongue
was the language of a beating heart
Fluid
Washing doubt away
Kind

Now that the earth
is closer to my mother
than I am
I understand no language
except when
a small black bird with a red beak
pecks incessantly at my window.

Everyone is a shadow of someone else
when they come into the world

They must discover that other
And walk alongside them

But I, no matter where I search,
Cannot find mine.

I am a lonely shadow
Waiting.

It was dawn
When the soft hand of fog
brushed against my shoulder
I woke up
It had crawled into my room through
the crack in the window
with a load on its shoulder
it was pushing away the azure light in the room

It stood beside me
Smiled
And disappeared

On the table
I found a parcel of dreams yet to be dreamt
for the long and cold nights
that await me.

Separation
has crushed the bones of my soul

In our waking hours, we wait by a blind
  window
I am only alive in my sleep

Through the pinhole of the hidden wall
I watch the living trees
And dreaming of death
I go to bed

Before plants and animals,
I am ashamed I was born human.

I was robbed
of my self
You who has turned the earth
into the dreadful dungeon of death

In utter darkness
You placed a pomegranate in my hand
that with its ninety arils,
might connect me to a dark hole

I am imprisoned within myself
in the depths of the earth

You have blocked all paths to light
Except the path of love.

Sunset's approaching
I bend to water the dahlias
Their colorful scents
attack
and seep deep into my lungs
I burst into tears
All my veins
All my muscles
All my bones
And the soles of my feet suddenly
swell so much
you'd think they want
to separate from the earth
gravity weakens
and I fly
It's painful
After flying my heart beats slower
As if I have died a little

In the beginning
Birds sang just as beautifully
as after humans named everything
The unnamed nature was just as beautiful
as it is now

Naming was a cruelty that endured
Giving birth to our needs.

After human extinction
Nature will be rid of being named
and it'll forget
the being whose love of nature
was cruel and destructive

I pull out
the fog from under my pillow
to immerse the room in mystery

Then, words
take me to a silver dream
and keep me there
until
curiosity comes alive in me

As though I am separating from everyone
I circle around dawn
I circle around myself
so that love awakens in me once again!

The Seven hidden doors
The Seven bright eyes

The Seven inconspicuous stairways
Where are they?

I pull out
this faithless body
from the depths of my soul

I tear apart
this inert cover
wrapped around my being
I escape from the narrow cage of flesh

Upward
Towards the star of darkness
that once was my mother
I ascend

Upward,
To the love beyond time—
Bodiless,
Alone.

The bricks of this room are made of love
You move through it—
with body, without body—
In search of healing,
In search of being understood,
In search of a cure for old wounds.
The magic of this room
has the rhythm of a cradle
Your search for
a fresh breath
to become yourself
It unwinds the yarn of sorrow
It shows that
truth is beautiful in its own right
This room bathes
in its own wellspring

When snow falls
and falls
I, like a delicate small plant
take refuge under a white sheet
But snow's attraction
is like that of moonlight
Even death is dressed in white
Ah—the weeping of this room is from
the dread of love!

From the Collection

I Can't Fall Asleep in This Doorless House

Sweden, 2018

Love

I fold the sheets of silence
for the days
when sound is absent.
Love is cloaked in fear
and lost its way

Silence is malleable
It pours
Cleans up
Spreads
Turns into a knife
and cuts.
It hides
It deceives
It dies,
It wakes up
It dances.

Silently,
it stands on the brink of wakefulness
and from within
It tickles my heart.
Silence is my friend:
It turns into a sheet
It becomes an embrace,
It rocks me,
It calms me.

Birds

Like black spears
The birds of dawn
pass by the window of exile.
They pierce the flesh of clouds
and circle back.
Blood
drips from my chest
onto the broken frame of
the image of a long-lost love

Spring

Spring has arrived
I, falsely,
feel young

I wipe the invisible dust
with an invisible cloth,
and in an invisible mirror
I see myself–
circling my youth

Spring has arrived
Long ago
I divided my skin
stretched it over
the bodies of my two children
so they might be
a piece of me
To clothe the future
in familiar clothing
Spring has arrived.

Stranger

Forget
where I was born
I, too, have forgotten.

The earth that swallowed
the body of our mothers
is akin to the earth
that covered your fathers.

Forget where I've come from
When I return to dust,
I will be no different
from you,
who are dust already.

The Moon

It's a drop of milk
dripping
from the open mouth of
a newborn galaxy—

Yet has never fallen

Self

Take off the mask,
so I open the door.
I've been waiting a long time
to return home,
unmasked,
to open the door on myself
and take myself
into my own embrace.

For a long time
I've been lost to myself,
I am distant
and I have lost all the signposts.
Will I recognize myself
if I return?

Wailing

How sorrow
hides under the carpet

Some days, this room is a house of mourning
Shrieks dripping, drop by drop.

I walk around in circles
and wail
the cry you taught me
in the cradle

Some days time is so deceitful
that the room burns with fever from sorrow

Some days time slithers inside me
until our faces merge as one.

In this ancient, alien room
I slowly
Disappear

Some days the poem resembles me so closely
that I no longer need a mirror

Return

The world was filled with cities
yet in none of them
did I have a home

Filled with beds,
yet on none of them
could I rest

Filled with streets,
yet in none of them
did I see a familiar face

We regress,
Slowly, slowly
we are returning
to primal savagery
to raw cruelty

There's freedom in ignorance
and haste in the return
to times without tenderness—
Circling the masochistic orbit of religion.

Twirling

The butterfly whirls in a trance
Twirls around the light
Twirls
Its delicate skirt quivers
quivers

I circle the butterfly
The room circles us,
All alike,
in an eternal rotation
we become planets
newly found
orbiting in delight

Upon dawn's arrival
without knowing
we have been pinned to eternity's wall

Flight

The dervish whirling
on the mantel in my room
wears a skirt of glass
and has left his heart
behind in Bukhara

This year, dark purple
is the color of the sleeping veranda
of my house.
In the suitcase leaning in a corner of the room
a letter rots
a house shifts
breathes with difficulty
but doesn't fall apart

Tie my wings.
Cut them.
The thought of flight
paralyzes me.

There's nothing left to see
Neither from above
Nor below.
The earth's dress
is a colorful lie
And I, from the beginning,
have remained naked

I Didn't Return

I was alone.
The mountain placed its breast in my mouth.
The river
braided my hair

I was alone.
Words came out of
the cracks in the wall

Man was dead to me
when he killed his neighbor

I was alone.
The bird took my poem
in its beak
and flew away.

Question

Old women
together,
alike,
with the same stride
in awe of everything
they walk slowly.

Their lips move
They answer each other
without hearing
the question

Poetry

Instead of crying
I composed poems,
Instead of screaming,
I wrote.
Instead of tears,
letters rained
from the corner of my eyes

I cried
and it became a poem
My outcry became a poem
My silence became a poem

Sometimes poetry
shut my mouth.
Ah, but only poetry
ever understood
how I felt

Poem

Last night a new poem
came to the window of my mind,
And even thumped against the glass.

It came—
But before I opened the door,
It vanished

The entire night,
in the sleepy alleys of my mind,
I searched for it
it wasn't there.
Without the cover of words,
naked
it was lost somewhere.

At dawn
I fell asleep in despair
hoping it might return.

Prison

We, the inmates
are imprisoned
for a crime we never
committed.

And our only arbiter
judge
and warden
is called God.

Truth

People
are one another's image
And don't know it.

Brains
filled with letters and numbers—
Futile
Fearful

And truth,
for centuries.
has hidden somewhere
out of fear.

Journey

The mountain that had hidden in my suitcase
was silent.
The ocean sheltered beneath my heart
heaved with waves.

And the forest
entwined around my shins
was growing taller

I took my mountain
out of the suitcase,
The ocean
from the corners of my eyes,
And I spread the forest
over strange lands
whose acquaintance
I longed to make

When the plane landed
the journey began.

Alive

From thought
to word,
From word
to sentence,
From sentence—
with a daring leap
unto the white surface of the page.

And again
Heading to the heart
To the ear
Splash
Splash
Splash
The caress of each syllable
In the veins
In feelings
And the deep delight of creation
And landing in poetry's embrace

For many years my being revolves around
these orbits
Revolves
and keeps me alive

The Room

On this journey
I turned you into the shape of a room
Rare
Timeless
Mine

I crawl inside you
Lean against your wall
Sleep on your floor
Inhale your breath
Dance in your mouth

On the hinge of delusion
I swallow your outcry
Walk in your dreams
Arrange your words on the floor
and sleep naked on them
And all that I have not told anyone
I whisper in your ear

From now on, you are where my life resides
O room filled with hugs,
Filled with ceilings
Filled with walls
O heart's mute confidant.

. . .

A mountain in love
scatters sparks

The earth's smile is green
The earth's mother weaves a garden

When the plain falls in love
It bursts into bloom
And we—
What do we do with love?

Language

My language is beautiful
Because my mother, with her whispers
Caressed me
Put me to sleep
Called me

Everyone
All over the world
For this reason alone
Keeps their language
Alive.

. . .

Does he come into my dream
or do I travel into
Nothingness?

From the Collection

Dawn's Door Stood Ajar, I Went Inside and I Have Still Not Returned

Sweden, 2012

To a Woman

This is your head
with two long braids
This is the part of your hair
Henna Colored
Saffron Colored
Wounded
Flower scented.

What is your head doing
in the midst of my dreams?
Your head still dizzy
from a man's blow
It is midnight
I have lost your face
You are my mother
the mother of mothers before me
You show
I see
A seven year-old boy
pounds on my dream's door
with the callused fingers
of a seventy year old
Staking his bright eyes
as a pledge.
in the desert of my dreams
What are you doing there,
night after night?

Self

I have pitched a tent within myself,
Drunk from the wine of my own making.
I have given birth to myself,
Nursed myself.
I am indebted to no God.
Time alone
 is the bedrock of my being

Where are you?

You reach out your hand,
Cut a sliver of the moon,
Lay it by my pillow
and fade away in the darkness
Forever.

Moon on the neck
Moon on the brow
A pulsing moon inside my heart—
I become
A wanderer in the world

This light has driven me mad;
Nobody dares
to make my moon whole anymore.
Where are you?
Where are you?
From within my piece of the moon
I call your name—
Find me
Find me.

Waiting

Venom drips
from the lip of the forest—
It is wounded

At midnight
the moon kisses
the soft shoulders of the mountain

A man in search of love
Between mountain and forest
Sharpens his axe
with words

To Stone

Which one of you
will I turn into?
You mute stones,
Your silence frightens me

I know you endure,
You witness
You carry secrets

Tell me—do you ache for my heart?
Do you resemble a God
born silent,
when you watch me
without eyes?

Small, But...

Bring your cheek close,
Very close
Closer still.

Receive the word
that turns like a stone
under my tongue
and will not fall out.

It is small,
Yet it will shake
the four pillars of the world

Familiar

I stand in the street.
Death tiptoes
behind me
with the face of an old fool.

Under my feet
the asphalt breaks into sudden weeping.
I turn around
and there you are,
coming toward me.

There's no escape.
Between you two—
Two infinities, unlit, without an opening—
I remain bewildered.

Dawn's door stood ajar
I went inside
I have still not returned.

The Turn

First to die were the books
in this house,
though they did not want to die.
Then it was the turn of living things.

I stood in a line
where I could not find myself,
Waiting, shifting from foot to foot,
where beginning and end were one.

Beneath the earth's wrinkled skirt
blind mice waited their turn,
until in an instant
they shred
gnaw to the bone
the one who was a stranger,
not of their tribe, and could see—

Once the books had died
forgetfulness rose
as a devastating wind.

Ode to Spring

Spring drips
from the index finger
of an old cloud.

My yard
in the thimble of a faceless woman,
brims with freshness and dew.

I am wandering
I am April
I am a stream
I am the Simorgh
who has lost my mountain.

In which celestial teahouse
did I drink unsweetened tea?

I lean the fallen ladder
towards the sun,
against a bare wall
once again
And I climb.

Time

When I last laid eyes on Time,
it was dressed in black,
trying to hide its wounds.

But It hid me
inside a hungry hollow
and asked me to wait.

The Last Word

With tired legs
Down the mountain he came
It was god
who longed for himself.

Secret

The original home was made of glass.
This is not our true place.
Sew my lips shut if I lie:
I will not die until the mystery is revealed

The fish have been promised my scattered
   particles
by the storm.
We will gather there, once more,
Intertwined,
Become a body there,
Find a new form
Be created from ourselves
within ourselves

Here, in protest,
Day lifts its skirt
And shows the earth
its shame.

From the Collection

Bitter River, Keep Me Alive!

Sweden, 2008

Where is my country?
I am the nation of loneliness,
With a displaced name
And borders that like wounds
fold inward

Where am I to be sold?
In which language
should I cry?

Bitter River—
keep me alive!

Poet's footnote: In Assyrian tablets, the Persian Gulf was referred to as the Bitter River.

Confession

I'm of the People of the Pact
I'm *ajam*
I'm mute.
I'm an idolater
I'm an infidel
I'm an apostate
I'm an atheist
I'm a heretic
I'm a rogue
I'm a rogue
I'm a rogue, a rogue.

I was born before you.
You were not yet born
when I was carved into
the threshold of the temple
and water and sky were under my command.

You built a shrine on the crown of my head
And the drought never left us

You cannot break me
I'm no longer of marble.
I'm of skin and bone,
I'm of words
I'm of truth—
I'm human.

Kneel before my heart.

It Hurts

You stand on the edge of another heart
and you kill yourself.
On the swell of feeling, as you rise
you crash.
Every time,
Always.

It hurts

The abyss is within you—
We hear only the sound of your falling
And that heart, your precipice
is left to mourn forever

I don't know,
I don't see,
I can't even imagine
how each time
you are born again.
Who is your mother, really?
Where is she?

Perhaps you are
the transpiration of an ivy vine
Born of a shell

Crawled out of a stone–,
Or spewed by a whale
toward the shore
in the dark.

Who knows?
Perhaps the sperm of a fish,
conceived in the privacy
of cave and cow.

Each time, after appearing,
you promise to stay
Stay down there—
Hold fast to the hem of my skirt,
Weave dreams,
Bear your heartache
down there.

On the thin stitches of my dress
Write,
Pitch a tent,
Make a home.

You can't tolerate

(continued on next page)

standing atop the fierce heights of your feelings
At such altitude
Love has a different color,
It's breathtaking
Even if all the planets of the cosmos
were filled with air
and blew it toward you
still you would flutter,
suffocating.

Stay.
Lean on the slopes of your emotions
Recline
against the softest muscle of the world.
You are freer
when you take refuge beneath your passion.

Know this:
At the zenith
Love only delays death
a little.

Love

The night is filled
with its own darkness
The sea with its own waves
The woods are filled with roots
The prisoner, his own poison

But the heart—
This vast void
This vessel nested within vessel,
This empty solitude
With what shall it be filled?

If we had known,
Love would have never been so repetitious

It has a thousand angles,
A thousand faces,
A thousand names,

And yet each time it knocks,
It comes as a stranger—
Faceless,
Seeking its own image
Clawing at your heart.

That Night

Last night I gave birth
to twenty-four thousand men
with small skulls.

Or perhaps it wasn't last night—
It was the night when the gates of time
opened upon the earth
There, at the eternal, unfamiliar, unexamined bend
My head swelled with illusions.

My sons took to the desert,
with their small, stunted minds,
Hungry,
Alone—
And gave madness
a new name.

Tomorrow night
I will bury them all.
Wait.
Bring shovels,
With a cloak of intelligence,
To the desert
The wilderness,
The plain,

The mountain.
We must bury them all

I long for the daughters
I did not give birth to
on that azure night.

Do Not Throw Stones

Each naked sheet of paper
I set on my knee
and dress with love.
I have sewn,
I have woven,
I have spun,
I have spun—
Suitcase after suitcase
Bundle after bundle.
This was all I knew
All I could do.

Let me be
In this straw room
I have settled in my solitude.
On this mad planet
Do not throw stones
My body is made of mountains;
I will not fall
I will not die

Do not blow
I will not turn to smoke
I am sitting on a stoop that reeks of blood
All my journeys have been in this room

Do not curse me
I gave my heart to no prophet,
I trusted none.
My sense for the smell of lies
is keen

When you blow, I tremble
Yet gravity
Beneath my feet
grows so dense
that invisible fingers
thrust from the stone
to hold me in place.
The wind will not carry me off
I am carved into the rock.
When you poured the ocean of terror
into my room
my lungs became whale-like.
No, I will not drown
I will stay in this room
until I become light

Wrath

I'm a fixed star
in this room
that is my future,
beside this table
that is the crucible of my imagination,
and in this dress
that was my youth.

I circle the particles
of feeling and speech,
I spin a web,
I spin a web,
and I become my own prey

Even now
On all the dark streets
In all the narrow corridors,
and in all the sparse rooms,
The wind is blowing.
The shiny dagger of thunder
scars the modest face of the sky.
The seal stamped on the arm
of the lover tree
burns it down.

Mad for light,
at last becomes void of itself

And every night I bow down
and kiss the innocent soles
of the earth.

Enlightenment

The rope chokes,
It drags the trunk of love
down from the heights,
It twists,
It writhes—
Gallows, gallows, gallows.

Bring the bodies down,
Count them,
Count them.
On the delicate throat of love
the rope leaves a trace
Unbind her hands
She wanted to write

I weave
You tear
I sew
You shred.

Truth was wound tight in rope,
So dream might stroll in peace,
So mystery might come to be,
So imagination might gallop unbridled,
So God
might be created.

I nursed
I applied salve
You inflicted the wound

I sang
You howled.

I inquired
You invented prophets
I inquired
You showed me hell.

You waged war,
I gave birth.
War was your pastime,
Love was my window

Calm down
No more time remains
Your mirror is in my hand.

Look
Look
This is your reflection.

I Stomp My Feet

I stomp my feet,
I stomp my feet—
One day,
Two nights,
Three months,
Five years,
Fourteen centuries.

I stomp my feet
in frustration
with intention
in anguish
in my room
in my grave
in my past
in my future
In my mother's womb,
I kick up dust

I swallow dust
I turn to dust
I stomp my feet.

I wait
I wait.

Poetry and I

My refuge,
The shell of my soul,
The robe of my spirit,
The veil of my internal face

My home
A skin that envelops me,
Turns me into a fetus,
Peels the skin of my memory

And puts a spell on my days
This centipede of a mirror
crawls slowly towards death
bearing on its magical back
those dark lines.

Exile

The land of exile
is a land with many cracks
You must lighten the weight of memories
Or else
It makes no difference where you step
Finally one day
one of the cracks
will stealthy devour you.

Death

At the time of death
What difference does it make
which house I occupy
A cave
Or a bed of satin
In my homeland,
Or in a room in exile?
Only the one standing beside me matters—
Hold my hand.

Fālgush (Eavesdropping)

I stood behind the wall of wind
and listened to the water.
Behind the wall of water
to the song of wind.
Behind the wall of soil
to the whispers of plants.
Behind the wall of light
to the pulse of shadows.
And behind the wall of your skin
to the whispers of love.
But I understood
the language of none.

The End

I draw the curtains
I water the flowers
I write the name of the goldfish
in the glass bowl
on the wall
I put on my blue dress.
Then I go to bed
and die.

From the Collection

The Eighth Realm

Sweden, 2004

The Eighth Realm

It's afternoon
Seated in the eighth tier of my soul
I look down
at the cliffs
that always keep me suspended
between two infinite feelings—
Death and love;
At those lands
that would not give me back to myself,
And at the women
who stayed small
inside my veins

Here, in the eighth realm of the soul
Among clocks without hands
And calendars without numbers,
I sit, tearing seam by seam
the tattered garments on my flesh—
Until I am on the brink
of complete nakedness.

Poet

I dance,
I dance and I sing.

Hafez holds the hem of my skirt
Rumi smooths out
the pleat in my shirt,
and Khayyam
combs my hair with wine

I am the dancer of the world of words
Yet every night
I place my head on Hallaj's shoulder
and weep

I am a woman poet.

Poem

Gather your *ghazals*
from this plain.
Pluck your *roba'iat*
from the stalks.
Snap the thick branches
of the *qasideh*.
Separate
the crawling twisty *do-beytis*
from the lifeless, dead trees.

This plain is drying up,
And one day, from the weight of sorrow,
it will burn of its own accord.
And this small bowl of water
will not save poetry.

Dusk

The dusk of exile—
hard to bear.
Through the cracks of closed doors
it pulls its homesickness inside.

Whenever the room is brimming with dusk
I try not to inhabit my body
But sorrow
quietly follows me, tiptoeing
And in the half-light of memories
takes my hand
There is no escape
I stay to remember.

The dusk of exile—
hard to bear
The smell of cowflesh, sultry air, and unripe jujube
from the alleys of Ahvaz
clings to the white sheets.

Wild roses, dead too young
wither beneath the rain of chants and prayers
and scatter across the old carpet in the room.

The dusk of exile—
hard to bear
even if you are not in your body.

Wine

Each dawn
Returning from my walks
through dreams,
I leave the little door open
so the recurring nightmares can escape.

In the morning
A grapevines trellis,
under the heat of the sun,
reaches its ultimate ripeness
aware that death
waits for it, patient, still

Wine
Is longing in full bloom.

Stranger

We stood in an unfamiliar garden
Afternoon's scent drifted in—
The scent of afternoons of warm lands,
The scent of earth not yet
heavy with corpses.

We breathed, and wept.

In that alien garden
The trees did not remember us
And the birds, though they leafed through
the garden's memory
found no trace of our names.

The water's conscience was devoid of our image,
and the leaf's delicate tongue
 was unfamiliar with the taste of our skin

In the garden of strangeness,
we too were strangers.

Waiting

Waiting rises like a height,
with summit
and slope.
Patience is a plain,
Broad and open.
And longing
is a fine drizzle of rain.

I Am Free

I move away from you
I don't bend toward the abyss;
Nor hang from that height
to stare into the depths

You are the abyss
You are the hollow
You are devoid of yourselves,
You, even, rob me of my voice.

I move away from you
I am a particle
One with the wind.

Name and lineage belong to you;
I belong to life
I am the wind
I am free
from the five imperfect human senses,
from the treacherous octopus of pain

I move away from you
beyond the walls of perception
I am so slight
that no god now
deigns to take me seriously.

Revolution

The tree born before me
will outlive me
I eliminate gender from all things,
So we may take the shape
of the pain we endure.

Let the bi-gender sun
warm the earth—
What does it matter
which pronoun defines it?

The moon that shines in my poem
is neither woman nor man
But a pure infant of the sky

Language, spun out of thin threads
Destroys
the muscles of my truth
under constant pressure

We must open new doors
onto the garden of language
Deliver the myths
from the torment of sterility,
Lay god bare

And let the soul free
to choose its own clothes.

After my death
Scatter the dust of my bones
for the birds to eat
So that poetry will drip
from their beaks

My End

Night's mouth is soaked in sequin
The exhalation of love
is loneliness.
I have vanished in streets entangled with
themselves,
Knowing no alphabet of any tongue
In an elevator descending to the depths
a mirror hangs
revealing the grooves of the soul
I saw the world's five continents laid bare.
Clinging to a skyscraper
I picked a blade of grass that would poison
every prophet still to come.

Memory

He takes her hand,
Hesitant,
Compelled yet unknowing
She follows me.

I mean the tree
I take her hand,
And at the height of her physical maturity
I take her toward autumn

Her journey is circular.
She has no memory.
Cannot remember her pain.
She has forgotten the torment
of nerves torn from their roots
She steps into autumn
without objection,
yielding to decay

I sit upon the stump of my old age,
I remember,
And I wait.

From the Collection

The Red-Dressed Woman That's Me

Sweden, 2001

My Calendar

Days go by
Without my knowing
Their calendar of origin
Their abyss of destination

But my day
Starts from within me
And my night starts
With sorrow
Conquering my heart.

Come visit me
At a time
when I have not yet
been thrown from the cliff of day
to the bed of night

Come visit me
Knock twice
on the door of my loneliness
Step into my land

I am of word and stone
Of plant and light
And for a thousand years
I have been longing for you
Come visit me.

The Red-dressed Woman That's Me

In memory of Babak Khorramdin,
seeker of peace and justice

From the mountains of bewilderment
I look at you
From the top of the azure mountain
I whisper your name
Seven thousand times—
In solitude
In a crowd
In a foreign city
Until your mythical courage
returns again
to my veins.

I am a red-robed God
Seeking justice
I have forged a sword of love
And a prophet of words
I wear a robe of wisdom
And my dream
Is giving birth
to someone like you.

The Desert

The blue veins of the sky
have swollen.
The capillaries of the moon's breast
and the green veins of the trees
have swollen

Thirst
is the nature of the soil
And the covering of human heart
is made of desert clay.

The Bird

From the tender, delicate branch of spring
I jump
into the clear cradle of summer leaves
And from there, rapidly
into the colorful rivers of autumn

And then
I stand
in the calming winter dawn
and anxiously
search for my memories

I cannot find any trace of the sun
among my feathers
And the cold reminds me
that I am a guest-bird
Exiled

And my brief being
in this land
finds meaning
only by finding a friend
A companion in flight.

The Sorrow of the Earth

The tree
shoulders the earth's sorrow
The clouds that of
the winds
And humans
that of the clouds.

In the small house of the self,
In the depth of the heart,
We carry
the sorrow of the world.

Temporary Home

I haven't yet
hung my curtains.
My windows are bare
I still imagine
I may not stay here for good.

But my homeland still
remains beneath
the weight of darkness and violence
And I don't want
the windows of my house
to conceal my loneliness
I don't want
the temporary safety of this house
to make me forgetful

For years
I wake up old
Next to you
I ask you my name
and wash my face
with your kind words

For in my homeland
Madmen
Riding the sterile horses of ignorance,
And the law
reeks of power and death.

The Secret

The mountain
hides its cry
buried in its heart.
The sea hides its sorrow
And the woods
the horrifying mystery
it has inherited
from the rotten body of man

Springwell

My journey
from the adobe house
to the closest
spring
took
a thousand years.

My thirst
dried inside the clay jug
And my haste in quenching my thirst
drove the wellspring
farther away still.

With the clay jug on my shoulder
and my thirst in my fist
I set out.

My skirt was old
My innocence worn thin,
My legs were weak
with the delicate muscles of habit.
And my affection
whose depth and breadth
I admired
found no buyer
in this land

The magical wellspring
I searched for
Had dried–
Forever.

From the Collection

Pari-Struck

Sweden, 1996

Iranian

My dinner plate
is Japanese.

The dress I wear
was sewn in Taiwan
by my half-hungry sisters.

My words
are stitched with the throats of Arabs.

My window opens
onto the green monotony
of a foreign land.

And only—
My soul,
My soul,
My soul—
Is insanely Iranian.

The Birth of Mithra

Naked I came,
Crowned not with thorns
But with ivy,
toward you.

Born of the aromatic core of a lotus
Of boulders
Of shells
Of the eighth realm*
And light was my name.

With my soul on my shoulder
I went, naked, toward the moon–
to surrender
to surrender
to surrender.

And my old body
was left behind
at the first gates of the world

Naked, I was coming toward you—
From the resurrection of my flesh
And my name was no longer
human,
No longer
human,
No longer
human

Referencing the mythological birth of Mithra.

Another World

My days go by
Soft and sorrowful
Soundless and secretive
and like a drop of water in snow
they disappear.

Love, with its azure eyes, stands waiting,
knocking at my window
But I am blind.
My eyes are dead,
and I am not ready to open the door.

I am mute,
and I have stowed away the pure unsullied words
for another world.

Refugee

I am a traveler in my own body,
a refugee within my soul,
a resident of a land
both kind and cold.

I have pills for my old pains—
yellow ones for vertigo
orange ones for unexplained fatigue
for loneliness, for forgetting.

But for the true affliction of my soul—
For exile,
For the old wounds of being human—
There is no cure.

A Small House

I have a small house
In a small town
In a small country

I am a small person
In a small world

One night, the stars
fell from my basket of carelessness
and covered
The fable of the world's fate

I have a lapis-blue bed
that my dreams warm
with your name.
I have an old unreadable book
signed by God

Listen to my voice
The voice of a woman
on whose heart
a heavy snow has fallen

I also have a small secret
that no trusted safe can hold

I will tell you
I will tell you

Only if you sit next to me,
and do not ask my name.

Stay by My Side

Morning birds
Cross-stitch the thin edge
of my morning slumber
with their songs

You pressed sequins of kisses
on the tips of my breasts,
And I, in the depths of my mind
dusted the old words of dreams

Your smile
Is the warmth of my bed,
Your gaze
the world's most soothing painkiller.

You calmed
the storm
of my body,
and upon the ancient wound
of my soul,
You laid your healing hands.

Stay by my side
Stay by my side
until my fingers
grow old within your hands.

Stay by my side
until history
believes in me.

In That Language

Don't let sorrow
be the conqueror of my night
Bring me wine
in a cup woven of gentle weariness and fatigue.
Sit beside me,
and speak to me
in a language I do not know.

Don't let grief
weigh down the sunsets of my home.
Bring me wine.
Sit beside me
and speak to me
in that language
from which I have been estranged
for thousands of years.

Fill my cup
and speak
Speak—
In that language I never learned in the cradle,
Speak,
Tell me
that you love me

My Homeland

I have built a room—
Of ruby, of root
Of pomegranate and thought.

I have built a room in exile,
A room of word and light,
A room of crystal—
A room that has become my homeland,
my sun, my sea, my earth

Yes—this room
is my homeland
and my grave,

A room built from the bricks of your land.
A homeland whose window opens
toward your house,
and yet remains unseen by you

At sunset
When I step into my land,
My body warms
with the heat of history and words
And my supper simmers
on a fire of patience and disregard

Pari-Struck

Neither of humankind,
Nor born of demons—
Small creatures,
Base,
Pitiful–
All body, stomach,
Color-blind too

Their vocal cords vibrate
only with the power of deceit.

Creature
without memory,
without love,
without affection—
They are jinns, no doubt
whose nightly attack
blindsided my homeland
No sound of footsteps
No sound of breaths,
They came like thieves,
And like poisonous rain
poured on our past and future history.

They came—
A legion of jinns—
From between the pages of a cursed book
From deceptive words
Leaning on a structure
built upon the black stone of deceit.

Now we the bewildered jinn-struck
Pari-struck and sorrowful
For even the chance to choose
has been taken from us.

From the Collection

The Moon and the Eternal Cow

Sweden, 1993

The Refugee

Let me wash his feet
Dress his wounds
Keep him awake
Let him
remember the name of his homeland
Let him
spit out the pain circulating in his blood
He, who like bones of ancient dead
is carried with the wind

Let me wash his wounds
Let me ask his name
Let him recall every bit of his nightmares

Let him set foot in your children's dream one night
Keep him awake
Keep him awake
So that I don't forget the name of my homeland

Tale of a Journey

Drops of sorrow gathered
through cold gray days—
So many, so heavy,
that through no opening
could I reach a single dream.

Nothing we can do
Let's open the old suitcases
So old memories come alive
So the room
fills with noise and movement
So color
pours out
of the window crack

Let's open the suitcases
So the suns we folded away
between pillows burn once more,

So the loves embroidered with words
become legible
So that in this room,
beneath the hot breath
of ancient attachments,
we grow thirsty—

And in that thirst,
find ourselves and nothing else.

To find ourselves—
Wasn't that, after all,
why we began the journey?

Ember

It's
the second time
that I take the ember
And I escape
From my homeland
From my bed
From my cradle and my grave
This time
I brought the flower
To the land of ice
Maybe
In the host's cold memory
I can stay alive
Now, the fire and I, alone
The fire in the brazier
and I, in bed

Will I find myself aflame, ever again?
In the old oven of that hearth?

You

I am the whale
and the world is the sea–
A cold,
narrow,
small sea.

And you–
You are the fountain of breath
I release toward the sky
on the surface of the water
and stay alive.

Song

Trees, grey
Sky, green
I'm made of dust
And hum a song
no bird
in this forest sings

Roots

A small room
The massive chest
A white wall
And curtains that
recklessly surrendered to the wind.

Lively eyes
on a face chafed by loneliness
and a body
with no roots

Where are my feet—
My feet?
Where are my roots?
Find
My hidden roots
Or deprive me
of movement

I want to, once more,
take root somewhere,

To stand firm again
upon the earth
and find peace.

The Wild Pomegranate

In my homeland
Every wild pomegranate bush
keeps a secret death

Every bush hides
the secret heart
of a fourteen-year-old girl

When its blossoms flare like fire
And the heart
is ready to burst open
The girl breathes the secret of her soul
into the bushes.

Pomegranates ripen—
Blood-red, alone—

When the girl
is gone.

Each pomegranate seed carries the taste
of a fourteen-year-old girl's sorrow—
In my homeland.

Take Me

Let me in
on your fears
Take me to that old shelter
To the small, sparse room
whose windows open
onto emeralds and dreams.

Take me through the corridors
of your childhood body
to the safest moment in the world.

Hurry–
Shelter me.

I Wish

I wish I couldn't walk
I wish I were fastened to the earth
The safe earth
with roots old and ancient

They called me
from the depths
I was a horse
galloping toward illusion

I wish I were fastened to the earth
with roots as frail as grass
I wish I were grass
I wish I could not move

Separation

I
was left apart
from the flock of lambs,
yet
I did not remain a lamb.

I learned
that innocence
is the choice of a shameful death,
And solitude
the price of awareness.

I stood apart—
Now neither lamb
Nor wolf,
Only eyes that
see,
see,
see.

My Poems

I have wept
I have lived
my poems.

Words are my old wounds—
They dry up and fall off.

I have
wept my poems
in the depths of lonely nights
I have wept
I have lived
my poems.

Blindsided

Not in a wheelchair,
Nor in a bed,
Not on a street corner,
Nor in a hospital

I will die
where Death does not expect me,

At the very moment
when the pride of my being
burns brightest in itself.

I will call to Death.
I will blindside Death
so it may come as a guest
into my body.

I Will Rise

I will rise
From my own ashes
From loss
From nothing

I will rise
From among bones
Addicted to emptiness,
To darkness

I will rise
From muscles displaced,
Inert,
Within the expanse of
a nameless body.

I will rise
From a dream torn apart,
To catch fire again,
To shine
And to die

Kinship

The birds came
with their ancient sacs of fear

The birds came
with the old terror of cold
Of storm
Of rain and wind.

The birds came
In longing for our old kinship
In fear.

They could not believe
my fears had new names
Loneliness
Exile
And fear of mankind
Mankind,
Mankind.

?

I am a black stone,
A mute bird,
A delicate root
In the bitter waters of the world.

Spellbound
Hidden in a black cloak
I have slept for a thousand years.

I am stone
I am essence
I am God.

Break me,
and know me.

Adrift

I am adrift in the world,
My backpack heavy
with exhaustion and neglect.

I am adrift in the world,
My backpack full
of spears — of word and fire.

I am adrift in the world,
My backpack burdened
with instincts buried in fear.

Ah—
I am searching for a place
to set down, forever,
the corpse of a god
that weighs upon my shoulders.

Creation

From worshiping stones
We came to worship mirrors
We saw ourselves
And created God

From the Collection

Concealers of Fire

Sweden, 1991

Forgetfulness

For my children
who grew silent on this journey
For my self
claimed by oblivion
And for those
who stayed and died

All day
I carry a handkerchief
to wipe this mirror
of dust and fog.

All day
I want to remember a word
So that my children's nights
are no longer cold and eerie.

All day
I dream again
the dreams of nights long gone,
Yet the spirit of the word is lost

My children wait,
Their eyes wide open
while I, and the world,
Are lost to forgetfulness.

Hustle

On cold gray days
when sorrow runs deeper
than my courage stands tall
and not a single memory returns
to warm the small heart of this room

On days
when the city is hidden
under a cover of neglect and fog,
And speech,
cannot stand
the density of sorrow,

On these days
when the fear of death
forms deep wrinkles
on the delicate skin of the world,

I try
to teach you the pronunciation of my name
And to hide
the moon
beneath my pillow of loneliness

Instinct

Since the day
Old dreams
leaned against my weary pillow
and denied me my fantasy
This room has never warmed,
The fire has never flared.

Each morning
Wet shreds of instinct
Swung on the clothesline
And I did not know
Which to put on
to begin this journey.

There Is a House...

Far away
Far, far away
A place where water
is sipped from a cupped hand
And bread
is steeped in the scent of life

A place where the sea
is filled with the moon
And the forests with green poison

A place where
woman is a red stain
on the wall of desire
And man
spurs a crazy horse
toward instinct and power

Far away
Far, far away
The place where I was born
Fell in love
Remained a mother
And lived but a few moments

A place where no dream
remains hidden
A house stands
on its ancient legs
And doesn't want,
Doesn't want
to crumble.

Elegy for a Woman

If I were to unpack
this bundle
Your simple world
would turn upside down

For I come
from a different land—
From the nightmare of fathers
who dance in eternal mourning
for their sons.

I have crawled out
of mothers' dreams
who never
Not for a single moment,
were bare of their flesh

From a grieving world
A world of darkness and madness
I step into your dream

Let
this bundle
stay closed.

Ask my name
Let me be reborn
in the light
of your simple mind.

They

They fished beauty out of the sea,
Life
out of the forest,
And death
out of the wells of distance and doubt.

The thousand years of my existence
Were the moments
I sat beside your shadow.

Your clouds drifted through me
And I learned to weep
And I wept.

I Want to Remember

The world strives
to make me forget
But I want to remember.

One day, I stood
by a luminous window
on an unfamiliar street
and I could no longer find myself.

Where I had died, I didn't know.
Ah—
I want to recall
To remember.

I look into different mirrors
and still I do not find myself.

And this eternal struggle
to find a place in this narrow coffin
Leads nowhere.

Always

On the stations of ice
On the trains heading to the sun
On the roads wet with illusion,
You,
Always you
Stood.

You,
with different names.

Death

I picked
the magenta moon
from a rootless tree along the way.
The room exhaled with joy,
and some pieces of the sky
took shape on the curtain.

Words gathered in my body.
Death, in my bed,
sat waiting
And sorrow crawled up my arm.

All night long, gray walls
with bone-hard teeth lay awake.

And by morning no one remembered me
and the yellow moon in the pot of my body
had dried up in sorrow.

The Desert-Dweller

I have come from the desert
I am a desert plant
and my torn, mad veins
spray upwards towards the sun.

Say my name and pass through this lake.
Say my name and entrust my hungry children
to the sky.

The moon, its breast heavy with milk
Stands at my bedside.

Waiting

Put on a robe of illusion
and come to my desert.
Put on a robe of dust
and step into my mirror

I shine
and I wait.

Old Women

At the last station, with mouths open,
Half-blind eyes,
and empty, simple memories,
Old women
in shiny, spotless clothes,
With red lips
and the scent of perfume
seeping from the cracks of a dead desire.

Old women
With earrings of regret and sour cherries
Teeth, even-sized and rootless
Trembling hands
At the last station.

They,
who carry my old age!
They,
who are me
They,
who from beneath their warm breasts
let drip, drop by drop.
the remnants of dormant desire.

They board
Old women without a gaze
Old women without support
floating in the void of the soul.

And for them the past
is a distant lost memory
they will never recall again.

I Didn't Kill the Nightingales

I—
I didn't kill the nightingales.
It was they
who didn't come into my poems.
I didn't hear their song
because there was no garden.

No fragrance
of sweetbriars and narcissus
in streets thick with iron and fear.
I never heard
the nightingale's song,
nor the cypress, the gazelle, the hoopoe—
They did not come to my poems.

For instead of the garden
I saw horses
carrying the dead
And gardeners
turned into the guardians of the night's honor
Gardeners whose dreams
were devoid
of even the scents and names of flowers.

I didn't kill the nightingales.
When I came,
they were already gone.

Do you believe me?

The Draft

A thousand doors
remained open in my soul
and a thousand windows
half-open
to the sea.

And I was always cold.

Then the draft of your love blew,
in its passing, whirling dance
shutting the doors once more.

And now, again,
The fire and I
are ablaze
in an oven.

The Trees

Trees of surrender
Trees without memory,
Trees with fragile roots—
The wind
disturbs them
The wind changes them.

Sturdy trees
Ancient trees
Trees with distant memories —
They bend the wind
into their shape,
The wind
ensnared among them,
Crying, howling,
With no escape.

Trees
whose bodies
frighten the mighty winds
And whose wisdom
Keeps them standing
Alone, free, and upright.

The Catch

I hold a net
Expansive as the mind of all mankind.

I spread it open—

I come to fish for words,
For those words that never
found the courage
to appear.

Half-asleep words,
Beloved, pure,
Settled in the depths.

It's the dawn of the last day of the world
And the net
is so heavy
that I believe
that no one
has ever spoken the word
he needed,
longed for—
Never
Not once.

From the Collection

Reclining on the Chariot of Sorrow

Sweden, 1988

Homeland

I weep,
I weep
for a house
that I swept clean of dust
for a thousand years
but it was still not clean

I weep
for a house
where I breathed love
for a thousand years
but it was still not warm

I weep
for a house
where I cooked an eternal supper
on the fire of knowledge
for a thousand years
but still no one
was satiated.

I weep
for a house
that, in the end,
never became my home.

From the Collection

Fast Gazelles of Memory

Iran, 1986

Youth

A garden of
flower seeds of blood,
and radiant roots of nerves,
A garden of the strong muscles of love,
tall poplars of bones,
and restless butterflies of pain.

I don't pass through the garden—
I stand in it
My name is not human;
My name blows toward me
from some distant winter.

Dark sunflowers
are surrounded
by a thousand wandering suns
And in my dream, they burn.

Moments pass through my body
in your name.
Indeed,
Youth was a spark
that flared in the dark
And I saw blue eyes—cold
gnawing on my flesh with the teeth of love.

The wind that blows in this garden
has passed through the roots of my body
A wind like a desert of remorse

These spruce trees
that have always trembled
out of reverence for love
They know my name
They know it
But won't utter it.

My Body Is Blue

I am the lady of useless objects
Of lifeless objects that never wake
Futility trembling on the soft edge of their being

I am the lady of plants
that have died
And to survive
my children nurse on the delicate fibers of my
mind

Hand me a vessel of indolence—
I lie with whales
who pour the ocean in my veins
who let me free
in a pond of sin

I am the mad lady of a house
with radiant walls
where the bones of my loneliness chafe.

My body is blue
And each morning
I hitch my boat of sorrow to the sun
so the hungry children
will not witness
the restless circulation of my blood
on walls, chairs and frozen sheets.

Children who comb my blue hair
with the sharp teeth of love
And with each kiss
tear the nerve of pain
within my body.

Meaning

The star rose out of the sea
It didn't walk on land
It spread its disheveled, delicate roots
in the sky

It unfurled the navy blue tablecloth
Stretched to infinity
And became our dinner guest

The star with its azure bowl
descended to the marrow of our bones
And stayed,
Stayed.
Stayed.

Until words, like fire,
sang the cry of love

The star fell in the water
And the words
carried us
to the depths of meaning.

It's Cold

It's cold
The tree throws its cover
in the direction of the wind
And the rustle of each leaf
foretells the sly passing of death

Only words—
Like a rain of stars and warmth
Fall upon the night of humanity.

The Voice

If I said sunlight
I would fall short of the night.

Darkness is a window
And loneliness pours onto the earth
from the sound of humankind.

Let us bend toward our solitude
Take the cold hand of the tree in the dark.

I have breathed my name into your fragile sleep
If you step down those high steps
And shake your eyes out into the night's dust
I will close this window
on the night's mischief.

The Illusion

Curious,
we pulled the curtain in the sky to the side—
No star
No sunlight—
Only a bed of navy blue
spread in the hands of our illusion.

On our skin
The unkind traces of time
passed casually
by the milk-white smirk of death.

And the sound of
humanity's song of pain
Brought the silent dove,
In the depths of the sky
to tears.

Astonishment

I die in the comfort of a chair
The room is empty
I've died

In death, we are all the same

All day long,
buses move toward an unknown destination
All day long
trains of terror
pass through my ears

Passengers, leaning on their newspapers,
look in astonishment
At their own faces
in the news reports

All day long
trains of terror
pass through my ears.

(excerpt from the poem "The Human Voice")

Still
In the throat of every newborn
There is an ancient sob
And a human's first sound is a cry
The likes of which
No sad bird
Has ever sung

Glossary

Ajam: A non-Arab; often used to refer to a Persian.

Bābak: A revolutionary Iranian leader (8th–9th century CE) who led a major uprising against the Abbasid Caliphate.

Do-beyti: A classical Persian poetic form consisting of two lines (four hemistiches) in which either the first and third, or the second and fourth hemistiches rhyme.

Eighth Realm: A mystical concept referring to the ultimate destination or heavenly realm.

Fālgush: A traditional form of divination practiced on the eve of Chāhārshanbeh Suri, the fire festival that precedes Nowruz. A girl stands behind a wall or around a corner, makes a wish or intention, and listens to conversation from passersby; what she overhears is interpreted as the answer to her intention.

Ghazal: A classical Persian poetic form of typically five to fourteen lines, in which the first hemistich of the poem rhymes with all even-numbered hemistiches.

Hāfez: 14th-century Persian poet, celebrated master of the ghazal.

Hallāj: 9th–10th-century Persian mystic and poet, known for his ecstatic utterance "*Ana al-Haqq*" ("I am the Truth").

Jinn: Supernatural beings in Islamic tradition capable of taking human form and possessing or influencing humans; often anglicized as "genie."

Khayyām: 11th-century Persian poet, mathematician, and astronomer, author of the *Rubā'iyyāt*.

Mithra: Ancient Persian deity associated with light, oaths, and cosmic order.

Pari: A graceful, supernatural being in Persian mythology, similar to a fairy.

Qasideh: A classical poetic form of at least fifteen lines, with a monorhyme pattern in which the first hemistich rhymes with all even-numbered hemistiches.

Robā'i: A classical four-hemistich (two-line) poetic form in which three hemistiches rhyme (first, second, and fourth).

Rumi: 13th-century Persian poet and Sufi mystic, author of the *Masnavi*.

Sources

Mossaed, Jila. *Penhānkonandegān-e Ātash* [Concealers of fire], Gothenburg: NashreDoosti, 2011. Pages 14-15, 19-20, 23,34-35, 39, 42-43, 48-49, 53, 56-58, 63-64, 71-72, 75-76, 82, 87-88, and 90-91. (first edition was published in 1991 by Navid Publishing in Germany and captures poems written in 1989-1990)

_______. *Māh va Ān Gāv-e Azali* [The moon and the eternal cow], Sweden: Arash Publishing, 1993. Pages 20-21, 25-28, 38, 45, 48-49, 56-59, 67-68, 73-74, 78-79, 86-87, 94-95, 98-99, 204-207, and 211.

_______. *Parizadegān* [Pari-Struck], Spånga: Baran Publishing, 1996. Pages 3-7, 21-22, 26, 31, 33, 35, 46, and 51.

________.*Sorkh Jāmeh-ee ke Manam* [The red-dressed woman that's me], Kista: Kitab-i-Arzan Publishing, 2001. Pages 5, 11-12, 15-18, 24-25, 32-33, 45, and 65-66.

________. *Eqlim-e Hashtom* [The eighth realm], Kista: Kitab-i-Arzan Publishing, 2004. Pages 13-16, 18, 42-46, 56-57, 71-72, 87, 90-91, and 93-94.

________. *Rud-e Talkh Zendeh-am Negahdār!* [Bitter river, keep me alive!!], Spånga: Baran Publishing, 2008. Pages 7, 10-11, 18-20, 38-39, 51-52, 59-64, 69-71, 76-78, 86, and 91

________. *Dar in Khāneh-ye Be-dar Khābam Nemibarad* [I can't fall asleep in this doorless house], Kitab-i-Arzan Publishing, 2018. Pages 11-13, 26-28, 31-35-38, 41, 51-54, 57-60, 63, 66-67, 70-73, 76-77, 87-88, 91-92, 99-101, and 107.

________. *Dar-e Sahar Nimeh-Bāz Bud Beh Darun Raftam Hanuz Barnagashteh-am* [Dawn's door stood ajar, I went inside and I have still not returned], Gothenburg: Nashr-e Doosti, 2012. Pages 18-19, 28-30, 37-38, 48-50, 66-67, 76-77, 87, 94, 100.

________. *Sogand beh Chehreh-ye Māh* [To the face of the moon] Kista: Kitab-i-Arzan Publishing, 2022. Pages 5, 8, 15-16, 24-25, 31-34, 37-38, 41-42, 49-51, 58, 66, 72-74, 77-78, 81-82, 87-88, and 94-96.

YouTube recitation of poems in *Ghazālān-Chālāk-e Khātereh* [The fast gazelles of memory]
https://m.youtube.com/watch?v=ukMmwNhtl9A

Jila Mossaed recitation of Homeland from the collection *Yaleh bar Kajāveh-ye Anduh* [Reclining on the chariot of sorrow]
https://m.youtube.com/watch?v=B8e6g8bAxrY&pp=0gcJCR4Bo7VqN5tD

Acknowledgments

One of the unique privileges of translating a contemporary poet is the ability to interact directly with the creator of the work. I was fortunate that Jila Mossaed generously sent me her books and was always available to answer my questions. Throughout this project, she was only a message away—a rare and remarkable gift. Working with her has been one of the great pleasures of this translation journey.

I am grateful to Mohammad Batmanglij, whose edits and suggestions have strengthened these translations many times over, and whose encouragement emboldened me to take creative risks in reordering certain lines to achieve a more natural flow in English. My heartfelt thanks as well to my aunt Najmieh, for her steady support and kind encouragement.

I owe deep appreciation to my daughter Tina, who has always made time to read the translations and offer insightful comments. I am continually in awe of her ability to spot typos and refine word choices I somehow missed after multiple readings. Listening to her observations—whether written or spoken—has become one of the most cherished parts of this process.

Finally, this book is dedicated to the memory of Claudette Sartiliot, who not only played a vital role in shaping my love of literature but also taught me about kindness, generosity, and unwavering support.

Other Mage Poetry Titles

Song of the Ground Jay: Poems by Iranian Women, 1960–2022
Bilingual Edition / Selected and Translated by Mojdeh Bahar

Milkvetch and Violets
Bilingual Edition / Mohammad Reza Shafi'i-Kadkani
Translated by Mojdeh Bahar

Faces of Love: Hafez and the Poets of Shiraz
Bilingual Edition / Translated by Dick Davis

The Mirror of My Heart:
A Thousand Years of Persian Poetry by Women
Bilingual Edition / Translated by Dick Davis

Vis and Ramin
Fakhraddin Gorgani / Translated by Dick Davis

Khosrow and Shirin
Nezami Ganjavi / Translated by Dick Davis

Layli and Majnun
Nezami Ganjavi / Translated by Dick Davis

Borrowed Ware: Medieval Persian Epigrams
Introduced and Translated by Dick Davis

When They Broke Down the Door: Poems
Fatemeh Shams / Introduction and translations by Dick Davis

Another Birth and Other Poems
By Forugh Farrokhzad, translated by Hasan Javadi
and Susan Sallée / Bilingual edition

Obeyd-e Zakani: Ethics of Aristocrats and other Satirical Works
translated by Hasan Javadi

Audio Books

Vis and Ramin
Fakhraddin Gorgani / Translated by Dick Davis
Mage Audio / Read by
Mary Sarah Agliotta, Dick Davis (Introduction)

Faces of Love: Hafez and the Poets of Shiraz
Translated by Dick Davis / Penguin Audio / Read by
Dick Davis, Tala Ashe and Ramiz Monsef

The Mirror of My Heart:
A Thousand Years of Persian Poetry by Women
Translated by Dick Davis / Penguin Audio / Read by
Dick Davis, Mozhan Marno, Tala Ashe and Serena Manteghi

The Shahnameh
Abolqasem Ferdowsi / Translated by Dick Davis
Penguin / Echo Point Audio / Read by
Dick Davis, Sean Rohani, Nikki Massoud

Khosrow and Shirin
Nezami Ganjavi / Translated by Dick Davis
Penguin Audio / Read by

Dick Davis, Peter Ganim, and Mozhan Nabavi

Layli and Majnun
Nezami Ganjavi / Translated by Dick Davis
Penguin Audio / Read by
Dick Davis, Peter Ganim, Serena Manteghi and Sean Rohani

My Uncle Napoleon
Iraj Pezeshkzad / Translated by Dick Davis
Mage Audio / Read by
Moti Margolin, Dick Davis (Introduction)

www.ingramcontent.com/pod-product-compliance
Lightning Source LLC
La Vergne TN
LVHW091634100826
845152LV00002B/33

* 9 7 8 1 9 4 9 4 4 5 9 6 1 *